Happy Holidays!
Veterans Day

by Betsy Rathburn

BELLWETHER MEDIA • MINNEAPOLIS, MN

Blastoff! Beginners are developed by literacy experts and educators to meet the needs of early readers. These engaging informational texts support young children as they begin reading about their world. Through simple language and high frequency words paired with crisp, colorful photos, Blastoff! Beginners launch young readers into the universe of independent reading.

Sight Words in This Book

a	in	people	this
about	is	the	to
day	it	them	were
go	may	these	who
help	on	they	

This edition first published in 2023 by Bellwether Media, Inc.

No part of this publication may be reproduced in whole or in part without written permission of the publisher. For information regarding permission, write to Bellwether Media, Inc., Attention: Permissions Department, 6012 Blue Circle Drive, Minnetonka, MN 55343.

Library of Congress Cataloging-in-Publication Data

LC record for Veterans Day available at: https://lccn.loc.gov/2022036395

Text copyright © 2023 by Bellwether Media, Inc. BLASTOFF! BEGINNERS and associated logos are trademarks and/or registered trademarks of Bellwether Media, Inc.

Editor: Christina Leaf   Designer: Laura Sowers

Printed in the United States of America, North Mankato, MN.

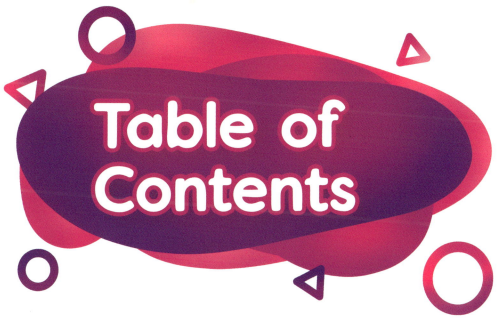

Table of Contents

It Is Veterans Day!	4
A Day to Honor	6
A Day to Give Thanks	12
Veterans Day Facts	22
Glossary	23
To Learn More	24
Index	24

It Is Veterans Day!

People fly flags.
It is Veterans Day!

A Day to Honor

The United States honors this day. It is on November 11.

A war ended on this day.

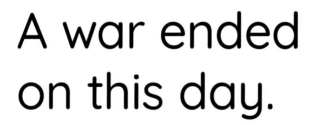

the day World War I ended

It honors veterans. These people were in the **armed forces**.

veterans

A Day to Give Thanks

People go to **parades**. Veterans may walk in them.

People show **respect**.
They cheer.
They wave flags.

People listen to stories. They learn about wars.

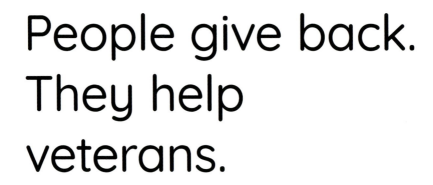

People give back. They help veterans.

This is a day to thank those who **served**!

Veterans Day Facts

Celebrating Veterans Day

veteran

flags

parade

Veterans Day Activities

go to a parade

wave flags

thank veterans

Glossary

armed forces

the groups that keep a country safe

parades

people or groups who walk together during events

respect

care for other people's thoughts and feelings

served

worked for the armed forces

To Learn More

ON THE WEB

FACTSURFER

Factsurfer.com gives you a safe, fun way to find more information.

1. Go to www.factsurfer.com.

2. Enter "Veterans Day" into the search box and click 🔍.

3. Select your book cover to see a list of related content.

Index

armed forces, 10
cheer, 14
flags, 4, 14
give, 18
help, 18
learn, 16
listen, 16
November, 6
parades, 12, 13
respect, 14
served, 20
stories, 16
thank, 20
United States, 6
veterans, 10, 11, 12, 18
war, 8, 16

The images in this book are reproduced through the courtesy of: ND700, cover; wavebreakmedia, pp. 3, 14, 22 (wave flags); fstop123, pp. 4-5; Cheryl Casey, pp. 6-7; Science History Images/ Alamy, p. 8; ESB Professional, pp. 8-9; aaron LeMay, pp. 10-11; Steve Sanchez Photos, pp. 12-13; Richard Levine/ Alamy, pp. 14-15; qingwa, pp. 16-17; Jim West/ Alamy, pp. 18-19; Bob Daemmrich/ Alamy, pp. 20, 20-21; Aleksandr Dyskin, p. 22 (celebrating); Popova Valeriya, p. 22 (go to a parade); Pamela Au, p. 22 (thank veterans), 23 (served); Bumble Dee, p. 23 (armed forces); Peng Ge, p. 23 (parades); flysnowfly, p. 23 (respect).